THIS WALKER BOOK BELONGS TO:

First published 1991 by Walker Books Ltd
87 Vauxhall Walk, London SE11 5HJ

© 1991 Jan Ormerod

Printed and bound in Hong Kong by
Sheck Wah Tong Printing Press Ltd

British Library Cataloguing in Publication Data
Ormerod, Jan
My little book of numbers.
I. Title
823'.914 [J]
ISBN 0-7445-0995-5
ISBN 0-7445-1473-8 Pbk

◆ my little book of ◆
numbers

Jan Ormerod

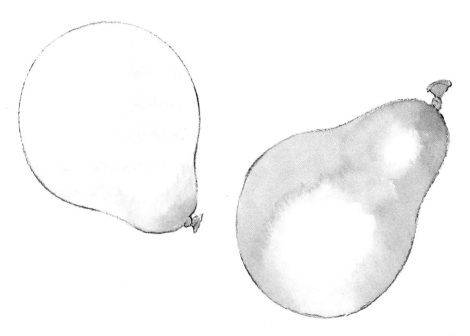

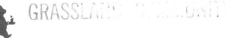
WALKER BOOKS
LONDON

1
one
candle

2
two
balloons

3 three
presents

4

four

cards

5

five

party masks

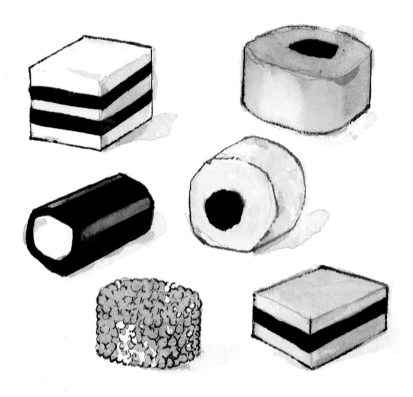

6

six

sweets

7

seven
party blowers

8
eight
fruit drinks

9
nine
ice-creams

MORE WALKER PAPERBACKS
For You to Enjoy

Also by Jan Ormerod

MY LITTLE BOOK OF COLOURS

Getting dressed is the activity in this
delightfully simple introduction to the concept of colour.

ISBN 0-7445-1474-6   £2.50

DAD AND ME

A father and his baby get to know one another.

"Gentle, humorous and true to life." *TES*

Messy Baby	ISBN 0-7445-0929-7
Reading	ISBN 0-7445-0927-0
Dad's Back	ISBN 0-7445-0930-0
Sleeping	ISBN 0-7445-0928-9

£1.99 each

**Walker Paperbacks are available from most booksellers, or by post from
Walker Books Ltd, PO Box 11, Falmouth, Cornwall TR10 9EN.**

To order, send: Title, author, ISBN number and price for each book ordered
Your full name and address
Cheque or postal order for the total amount, plus postage and packing:
UK, BFPO and Eire – 50p for first book, plus 10p for
each additional book to a maximum charge of £2.00.
Overseas Customers – £1.25 for first book,
plus 25p per copy for each additional book.
Prices are correct at time of going to press, but are subject to change without notice.